DON'T GET EATEN

The Dangers of Animals That Charge or Attack

Dave Smith

THE MOUNTAINEERS BOOKS

Published by
The Mountaineers Books
1001 SW Klickitat Way, Suite 201
Seattle, WA 98134

© 2003 by Dave Smith

Published simultaneously in Great Britain by Cordee, 3a DeMontfort Street
Leicester, England, LE1 7HD

Manufactured in Canada

Acquiring Editor: Cassandra Conyers
Project Editor: Sunny Monroe
Copy Editor: Julie Van Pelt
Cover and Book Design: The Mountaineers Books
Layout: Jennifer LaRock Shontz
Illustrator: Moore Creative Design
Cover Illustration: Ani Rucki

Library of Congress Cataloging-in-Publication Data

Smith, Dave, 1950–
    Don't get eaten : the dangers of animals that charge or attack / Dave
Smith.— 1st ed.
        p.   cm.
Includes bibliographical references.
    ISBN 0-89886-912-9 (pbk.)
1. Animal attacks—United States—Prevention. 2. Animal
attacks—Canada—Prevention. 3. Outdoor recreation—United
States—Safety measures. 4. Outdoor recreation—Canada—Safety
measures. 5. Animal behavior—United States. 6. Animal
behavior—Canada. I. Title.
    QL100.5.S65 2003
    796.5—dc21
                                                        2003001973

Contents

Introduction   7

Chapter 1. **Black Bears**   9
  Danger: Real and Imagined   9
  Black Bear Defense of Personal Space   10
  Black Bear Predation on Humans   11
  Avoiding Problems with Black Bears   13
  Rehearsals: What to Do in an Encounter   19

Chapter 2. **Buffalo**   25
  Injuries from Buffalo   25
  Hikers Beware: King of the Range   27
  Avoiding Confrontations   30
  If You Are Charged   31

Chapter 3. **Cougars**   33
  Where Are the Cougars?   35
  Avoiding Trouble with Cougars   35
  Kids and Cougars: Pretrip Planning   37
  Close Encounters: What to Do   37

Chapter 4. **Coyotes**   41
  The Danger Zone: Populated Places   41
  When to Be Wary and What to Do   44

Chapter 5. Grizzly Bears 45
Essential Grizzly Behavior and Biology 45
Safe Recreation in Grizzly Country 48
Grizzly Attacks Demystified 52
The Power and Perils of Pepper Spray 55
Encounters with Grizzlies: What to Do 60

Chapter 6. Javelinas 65
Javelina Social Life 65
Javelina Attacks 67
Javelina Encounters in the Wild: What to Do 69

Chapter 7. Moose 71
Avoiding Confrontations 71
Moose Encounters: What to Do 74

Chapter 8. Wolves 77
Key Statistics 77
Wolves and People: The Big Picture 78
Avoiding Trouble with Wolves 82

Chapter 9. Rabies 83
What Is Rabies and How Do People Get It? 83
Preventing and Recognizing Rabies 86
If You're Bitten by a Wild Animal 87

Selected References 91

Introduction

Don't Get Eaten will help you avoid conflicts and confrontations with potentially dangerous North American land mammals, and it explains how to respond to encounters in worst-case scenarios. In addition to covering bears, cougars, and animals that might eat you, this book discusses buffalo, moose, and animals that can hurt you. It also examines creatures like the javelina that are perceived as dangerous or aggressive.

Some fears about wildlife are based on common but erroneous beliefs. Everybody knows you're in trouble if you startle a nearby black bear with cubs, but this book gives you accurate facts and figures on injuries caused by female black bears with cubs. The truth will ease your fears, but *Don't Get Eaten* doesn't sugarcoat the truth. You can look at the statistics on wolf attacks and decide for yourself if you want to take the risk of camping with wolves. The information here gives you the means to take a calculated risk.

Sometimes people get in trouble with wildlife because they just don't know any better. After reading this book, you'll know not to approach a docile-looking buffalo. You'll know that dawn and dusk are dangerous times to take your children for a walk in cougar country. You'll know enough to avoid a lot of potentially dangerous situations.

But no amount of knowledge can take all the risk out of sharing the outdoors with wildlife. Hiking in grizzly country is dangerous and that's all there is to it. You have to wonder if people travel thousands of miles to hike and kayak where there are grizzlies despite the danger, or because of it. Wildlife is a big part of the appeal of wild country. With this book, you'll gain the knowledge required to interact as safely as possible with North America's most dangerous land mammals.

CHAPTER 1

Black Bears

IMAGINE THIS:

You've paddled a canoe to a remote backcountry campsite, and as you're setting up your tent, a black bear emerges from the forest just 40 feet away. The bear hesitates, and then walks directly toward you. Your response?

DANGER: REAL AND IMAGINED

People worry about being injured after startling a black bear on the trail. But from 1900 to 1980, there were only four documented cases in which people were injured after startling a nearby female black bear with cubs. People also worry about being injured when stumbling upon a black bear feeding on a carcass. Many hikers and hunters, after all, have been attacked after suddenly encroaching on the personal space of a *grizzly* feeding on a large mammal carcass such as a deer or an elk. At the 1993 Fifth Annual Western Black Bear Workshop, during a presentation on black bear attacks, a roomful of biologists was asked about such attacks. Nobody was aware of a single case of a person being injured by a black bear feeding on a carcass. Since then, there has been one documented case.

Food-conditioned bears seeking a meal in your camp are more problematic, although it must be noted that injures are uncommon, and serious injuries are rare. The serious issue, the real cause for concern, and the type of black bear you need to be aware of, is the predatory black bear.

Black Bears at a Glance

Males average 200–300 pounds, 5–5½ feet from nose to tail, and are 30 inches high at the shoulder, although the rump is the high point on a black bear. Females are about 20 percent smaller. Black or brown coloring is most common. Average speed is 25–30 miles per hour and black bears have short, hooked claws for climbing. Black bears' hearing is more sensitive than a human's, with a wider frequency range, and their sense of smell is legendary: They have one hundred times more nasal mucosa area than a human. Black bears see in color and have good peripheral vision. Vision from afar has not been tested, but there are reputable anecdotal accounts of black bears picking out moving objects at considerable distances.

BLACK BEAR DEFENSE OF PERSONAL SPACE

Every bear has a "personal space": the area around the animal that, if entered, will cause the animal to fight or flee. The extent of a bear's personal space varies with each bear and each situation. You might encroach on the personal space of a female with cubs resting in the forest on a hot day at a distance of 70 yards. The distance could be 40 yards for a male bear in a patch of ripe berries. When you intrude on a bear's personal space, the bear regards you as a threat. It might flee, or it might defend itself.

Many people regard black bears as mini-grizzlies and believe that if you're hiking along a trail in New Hampshire and you startle a nearby bear, it will charge and injure you. Not likely. If you startle a nearby black bear, it will almost always run away or climb a tree. Here's why. Black bears and grizzly bears have different evolutionary backgrounds. Black bears evolved in forested areas of North America, while grizzlies evolved in more open terrain. Since grizzlies often had nowhere to hide and no trees to climb, a female had to defend her cubs by charging predators and threatening intruders (see chapter 5, Grizzly Bears). Black bears are different. Rather than fight, black bears climb a tree or vanish into the underbrush. Black bears in the wild rarely charge people and make contact—even females with cubs or mature males feeding on a carcass.

When a black bear detects an intruder well in advance—which is typical—the bear generally ambles off in another direction. Sometimes black bears that sense intruders hide. Black bears are so good at hiding, they've been known to use a large tree as a visual screen while peeking around the trunk to watch a nearby person. The black bear's almost magical ability to disappear into the woods was beautifully captured in the title of a book by John Beecham and Jeff Rohlman—*A Shadow in the Forest: Idaho's Black Bear*.

WARNING

The black bear you need to be concerned about is a bear that is aware of you yet approaches and willfully encroaches on *your* personal space.

BLACK BEAR PREDATION ON HUMANS

Hundreds of people feeding roadside black bears have been nipped and cuffed and have suffered minor injuries, but major injuries are another story. When biologist Stephen

Herrero analyzed serious incidents, predation was the motive for eighteen of twenty deaths caused by black bears. These were not surprise encounters where a bear reacted to a violation of its personal space. These were cases where the bear deliberately approached a person and preyed on him or her. Wild bears, not roadside bears, were typically the culprits. In some cases, the bears preyed on people sleeping in tents or under the stars. More often, predatory bears came after people during the day.

Fact

Black bears that prey on people are usually healthy. They're not malnourished. They're not injured. No wild bear or captive bear has ever been diagnosed with rabies.

Behavior of Predatory Black Bears

Predatory bears make a silent approach. They're intently focused on their victim. Sometimes they approach boldly; sometimes they stalk catlike. They may try to use cover and circle behind you. Unlike a defensive bear, which might lunge toward you several times without making contact, a predatory bear gets close, rushes in, and grabs you. Fight back by any means available.

It's a mistake to think a predatory bear will appear to be angry or somehow warn you before pouncing. Predatory black bears don't make threat displays or behave like a defensive bear. A "blowing" sound is the most common low-level threat from a defensive bear. It might be accompanied by laid-back ears, clacking teeth, a quick lunge or short rush in your direction, and slamming the ground or slapping a tree. Predatory bears don't make a commotion like defensive bears because if they did, they'd go hungry.

> **Fact**
>
> Black bears don't raise their hackles (pilar erection). Black bears don't threaten by growling. Researchers who have spent years in the field in close contact with black bears note that they have never heard a bear growl.

AVOIDING PROBLEMS WITH BLACK BEARS
Roadside Bears

There are parks and various places in the United States and Canada where you have a decent chance of seeing a black bear beside the road. These are not tame bears. If they don't seem overly concerned about your presence, it's because they're habituated. Simply put, they're used to being around people. (Habituation is fully explained in chapter 5, Grizzly Bears). But their tolerance has limits. They might not require as much personal space as a nonhabituated bear, but they are wild bears, and they will "fight or flee" when you cross an invisible line and enter their personal space. You can't possibly know when you'll cross the line, and it's foolish to gamble that the bear will flee rather than fight. Common sense dictates that you should never approach a roadside bear. Don't even get out of your car. Roll down the window and take pictures or a video.

Hiking

If you're traveling in black bear country, there's rarely any need to make noise as you're advised to do in grizzly country. Hunters who mask their scent, dress in full camouflage, and tiptoe through the woods have difficulty ambushing a black bear, so it's unlikely a family of four walking along a trail will take a black bear by surprise. Black bears usually detect people first and leave the area. If you manage to startle a nearby black bear, the bear will almost always flee. The only time it might be prudent to make noise is if you know you're entering a patch of ripe blueberries or some other spot likely to have black bears. There's no need to yell or blow an air horn—a loud conversation will suffice. Better yet, periodically break a good size stick or branch. That's an alarming sound to black bears; they listen for it. They think it's another bear approaching.

Don't leave your pack unattended. Keep it with you on all side trips or hang it from a tree (see Food Storage, next page).

Hiking with children. If you're hiking with adults and children, always have an adult at the front and rear of the group. It's the person in the lead who's most likely to bump into a bear.

If you're hiking with adults and children, always have an adult at the front and rear of the group.

Dogs. It's best to leave your dog at home. Untrained dogs have saved their owners from bears, but unleashed dogs have also drawn bears back to their owners. If you insist on taking your dog with you, keep it on a leash. Check local regulations because, in some parks, even leashed dogs are not allowed on trails.

Problems in Camp

Many encounters with black bears occur in camp. To avoid these encounters, take care in selecting a campsite and properly store all food, garbage, and attractants. Food and odors attract bears.

Food Storage

Know the local food-storage regulations. In most parts of the country, you can deter black bears by properly hanging your food from a tree limb or storing your ice chest in the back seat of a locked vehicle—but these techniques won't work in Yosemite National Park, so the regulations there are different. In Denali National Park, backpackers are required to use bear- resistant food containers. Whether you're pitching a tent in the backcountry for the night, or staying in a developed campground on a road, know the local food-storage regulations. There will be places where you can do more than the local regulations require, but never violate the rules and do less. The rules are usually based on a long, sad history of people failing to secure food from bears, and "problem" bears being killed to atone for human sins.

Always store food properly. A bear will eat anything that you, your pet, or your livestock will eat. All food for livestock, pets, and people must be stored in a manner that makes it unavailable to bears. In some areas, agencies provide food-storage containers or devices for hanging your food. Use them.

In developed campgrounds, it's a good policy, and often the official policy, that food, cooking utensils, food containers, and coolers must be in a locked, hard-sided vehicle or trailer when not in use.

Don't give bears visual clues. In some parks, bears have learned to associate ice chests, water jugs, and even grocery bags with food. If you leave these items in plain view in a locked car, an experienced bear will break in. A bear can pry out a windshield or bend open a car door. Whether you're parking at a trailhead for a few hours, or staying overnight at a developed campground, it's best to keep food-related items out of sight. Put them in the trunk of your vehicle. If you don't have a trunk, cover them with a sleeping bag or blanket.

Hanging food from a tree branch: the counterbalance method. A large black bear standing on its hind legs can reach up about 9 feet. Black bears can't jump like Michael Jordan, but they jump well enough to add a little to that 9-foot reach. This is why it's important to hang your food a minimum of 10 feet off the ground—12 feet is better. You'll need 50 feet of rope, two stuff sacks, and a stick at least 6 feet long for retrieving your food.

Find a tree with a live branch at least 20 feet above ground. Put a rock or heavy object in a stuff sack, tie it to one end of the rope, and toss it over the branch and back to the ground. Toss it as far out on the branch as will support the weight of all your food, but at minimum 4–6 feet from the tree trunk; 10 feet is better. Make sure there are no limbs just above or below your branch where a bear could climb out and reach your food.

Divide your food into two evenly balanced bags. Tie the first sack on and hoist it up to the branch. Tie the second sack high on the rope, and make sure you tie a loop so you can retrieve your food. Store excess rope in this bag. Push the lower sack up with a stick until the sacks are even. They should both be a minimum of 10 feet above ground. To retrieve, put your stick through the loop and pull down slowly.

Keep a Clean Camp

Burn all grease off grills and camp stoves. Wash dishes after each use—black bear country is no place to leave dirty dishes lying around. Strain dishwater at least 100 yards from camp and from water sources; dispose of food bits properly. Dispose of garbage correctly. If you're in a developed campground with bear-proof garbage cans available, use them. In the back-country, secure garbage with your food until it's time to go and then pack it out.

Don't bury garbage. Burying garbage is generally illegal, and always ineffective; bears (or other critters) will smell it and dig it up.

Never dispose of garbage or food in a latrine. Bears will find it and destroy the latrine in the process.

Odors Attract Bears

Don't cook in your tent. Don't eat in your tent. Don't store food in your tent. Store food in resealable plastic bags or air-tight containers to help contain odors. Try to keep your tent, sleeping bag, and personal gear free from food odors. It's best to leave perfumes and strong-smelling cosmetics at home— too much perfume can mask your human scent. Don't sleep in the clothes you cooked in. Store cooking clothes with your food at night.

Unexpected attractants. Bears are attracted to the smell of camera film. Store anything with an odor, not just food, out of the reach of bears. Tobacco products, sunscreen, mosquito repellent, first aid kits, petroleum products (bears will bite fuel

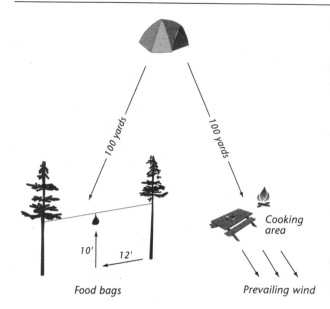

100 yards

100 yards

Cooking
area

10'   12'

Food bags

Prevailing wind

*Your cooking and food-storage area should be
100 yards downwind from your sleeping area.*

canisters), toothpaste, and more. Even nonodorous items will
pique the curiosity of bears—they've gotten into cans and
bottles of soda cooling in a stream.

A bedtime ritual. Check your pockets, fanny packs, and
gear for food and attractants. No gum, no lip balm, nothing.
Make sure there's nothing in your tent that might smell or taste
interesting to a bear. If you're camping with children, you can
make this important inspection into a fun game. Hide a candy
bar or some dried fruit in your pockets on purpose, and let
them keep what they find as a reward. (Just don't let them
sneak it into the tent for a midnight snack.)

Campsite Selection

Keep away from trails (bears use them day and night) and natural travel routes. Avoid berry patches and other seasonal food sources. If you camp in a noisy location—beside a fast-moving stream, for example—bears won't be able to hear you and you won't be able to hear them.

Sleep well away from food areas. It's wise to keep your sleeping area separate from your cooking/food-storage area(s). Some parks suggest keeping your tent site 50 yards away, others recommend 100 yards. The cooking/food-storage area(s) should be downwind of the sleeping area. Remember that cold air flows downhill at night.

Sleep in a tent. Bears usually won't enter a tent with a person inside, but there have been exceptions to this rule. There have been cases where bears bit people who were leaning against tent walls. If your tent is roomy enough, put your husband or boyfriend against the walls of the tent and sleep in the center. Seriously, put gear against the walls of the tent and sleep in the center. If you're camping with children, they're safest in the center of the tent. Adults should sleep on the perimeter.

REHEARSALS: WHAT TO DO IN AN ENCOUNTER

It's a good idea to rehearse what to do if a bear enters your camp, or if you encounter a bear on the trail—especially if you're camping with children.

A Black Bear in Camp: Nighttime

There have been a number of cases of black bears preying on campers at night. In some instances, the bears grabbed people sleeping under the stars. In other cases, the bears ripped into tents and went after occupants. Black bear predation on humans at night is rare, but it does happen. The bear's intent is to make a meal out of a human. It's best for adults and children to sleep in one tent so that adults are present to fight off any predatory attacks.

Mom, I have to go to the bathroom. At night, an adult should accompany children to the bushes, outhouse, or restroom.

Be prepared for predatory bears at night. Although it's highly unlikely a black bear will attempt to prey on you at night, it pays to be prepared. At the very least, keep a knife and a flashlight within reach. Some people are comfortable with firearms—but remember that firearms are prohibited in many parks. Make sure you comply with local regulations. And don't shoot your companions. (Pepper spray? See the discussion in chapter 5, Grizzly Bears.)

What to do if attacked. Fight back. Fight back with any weapon at hand, or your bare hands if need be. Fight back as if your life depends on it, because it does. A predatory black bear will not easily be deterred. If you don't drive the bear away, it will kill you and eat you. If you're engaged in hand-to-paw combat with a bear, direct your blows at the bear's head. Go for its eyes, nose, and ears. Children should be instructed to fight back if they're the ones being attacked.

A Black Bear in Camp: Daytime

If a bear that's aware of you still approaches and enters your camp, try to scare it away. If you have pepper spray, use it when the bear gets within range. Spray the bear in the eyes. (For a full discussion about pepper spray see chapter 5, Grizzly Bears.) If you don't have pepper spray, make loud noises, yell and holler, bang pots and pans. Throw rocks or sticks toward the bear. Take a quick step or two toward the bear and slam your foot down while clapping your hands—but don't get closer than 15 feet.

The more people creating a commotion, the more

intimidating and effective you'll be. Stand together, and don't surround a bear. Kids can join in, provided they stay behind adults.

A Black Bear in Camp with Your Food

This is not supposed to happen, but it does. Do you let the bear eat your food supply for the week, or do you try to scare it away? You can scare it away. A black bear is tougher to drive away once it begins eating your food. It might "blow" and make low-level threats. You might have to get closer than 15 feet. But if you're persistent, you should succeed in forcing the bear to retreat.

Fact

Black bears don't share food. A female doesn't present food to her cubs like a bird. If she kills a whitetail deer fawn, she immediately begins feeding. Cubs fight for whatever they can get. They fight each other, and they fight with their mother. If they yank off a leg or a big chunk of meat that can't be eaten immediately, they run off with it and vigorously defend their prize. This is why driving off a bear that's already into your food can be a bit dicey.

Black Bear on the Trail

You meet, both parties freeze for a moment, and then the bear walks toward you on the trail. Give the bear the right of way. Keep your eyes on the bear and step off on the downhill side of the trail. Give the bear room by quartering away from it (move away from the bear at an angle; direct retreat will embolden the bear). If it follows you, respond with the same aggression you'd direct at a bear approaching you in camp (see page 21).

Another scene: A nearby black bear sees you and approaches you. Its head is up; it's craning its neck and sniffing. It seems calm but its approach is slow and halting. This could be a food-conditioned bear, a curious bear, or a predatory bear. Act dominant. Yell. Throw something at it. Smack your walking stick on the ground or whack a tree with your hand. Don't retreat because the bear will only follow. Lunge at the bear and stamp your foot while clapping your hands. Increase the level of your response, as the bear gets closer. If all this doesn't drive the bear away, you're probably facing a predatory bear. Fight back if the bear attacks. Don't play dead.

Behavior Clues

✔ When a bear stands on hind legs, huffs, and sticks its tongue out, it's threatening you, right? Wrong. It huffs to exhale warm, damp air, which enhances its ability to gather your scent. It then uses its tongue and nose to analyze the information.

✔ Ears laid back—the bear feels threatened. Ears forward—aggression.

Sudden Encounter at Close Range

Don't run. Flight might trigger pursuit. It's especially bad for children to run because they are smaller and easier prey. Children should be trained to cluster around adults, but they should know NOT to hang onto your hand or arms.

Don't play dead. It could become a self-fulfilling prophecy. A bear that wouldn't approach if you just stood still might come over and injure you if you play dead.

Stand your ground. When the bear is stationary, quarter away from it. Don't turn your back on the bear. Keep watching it. If the bear approaches you, respond with the same aggression you'd direct at a bear approaching you in camp (see page 21). If the bear attacks you, fight back.

Sudden Encounter with a Female with Cubs

Pandemonium. The cubs scamper up a tree. The sow is "blowing" and huffing and clacking her teeth. Her ears are laid back. You can tell she's agitated. She lunges at you and slams her paws on the ground.

Stand your ground, then retreat. When the sow is stationary, retreat in a direction that takes you away from the tree with the cubs and the sow. The worst thing you could do is move toward the cubs' tree.

If attacked, do play dead. The only time it's appropriate to play dead with a black bear is when you're positive you're facing a sow with cubs and she rushes you and makes contact.

Tree Climbing

Climbing a tree to get away from a black bear is a grave mistake. One, you're always told not to run from a nearby bear because flight triggers pursuit; so running for a nearby tree is an error. Two, all black bears are far better tree climbers than people. They can scoot 30 feet up a tree trunk with no limbs as fast as a squirrel. Three, should you make it up a nearby tree and be pursued by a bear, you're in a poor position to fight it off. All you can do is kick at it. Black bears have grabbed people by feet or ankles and yanked them out of trees. Just the fall causes injuries, plus you've still got to contend with the bear when you hit the ground. Four, when black bears fight and one bear breaks off the encounter and bolts up a tree, the

Don't climb a tree to get away from a black bear.
The bear will pursue you and grab your foot or lower leg.

other bear reflexively pursues it. A black bear is far more likely to make contact with a person who climbs a tree than a person who stays on the ground and stands her ground.

Fifth, and perhaps most importantly, sows can lose track of their cubs during the chaos of a sudden encounter, and they get very, very, very disturbed by the sound of a tree being climbed. That sound tells them their cubs are climbing to get away from danger, or another bear is climbing after the cubs. If they see and hear you squirreling up a tree, and they think you're after the cubs, you're in trouble. One female black bear kept a national forest trail-crew member up a tree for over an hour. The man's co-workers had pepper spray, but he told them to stay away and they did. Dumb. The bear climbed up and attacked him again and again.

CHAPTER 2
Buffalo

> **IMAGINE THIS:**
> *It's mid-August, and you're walking through rolling, grass-covered hills in a western park when you top a rise and spot a herd of buffalo just 60 yards away. They seem calm and unperturbed by your presence. You notice a lone buffalo—a conspicuously big buffalo—about 200 yards away making a direct approach toward the herd. It's coming at an angle that will bring it within 30–40 yards of you. Is it time to skedaddle, or is it time to dig out your camera and move a little closer for some good photographs?*

Buffalo don't get the respect they deserve. They're remarkably tolerant, but they're also huge, powerful animals, well equipped for battle and capable of remarkable physical feats. Biologists in Alaska saw a full-grown bull leap over a 7-foot-tall fence from a standing position. Buffalo gallop at speeds of 30 miles per hour. They have massive skulls, and both males and females have horns used to "hook" and gore rivals, predators, and people who get too close.

INJURIES FROM BUFFALO
A study in Yellowstone National Park found that from 1982 to 1999, buffalo injured far more people than grizzly bears did. Grizzlies injured 32 people, including 2 deaths. Buffalo injured 81 people, including 2 deaths. In 1987 alone, buffalo injured 14 people. A big part of the problem is that people don't respect buffalo the way they do bears. We regard grizzlies as ferocious predators, while buffalo are seen as peaceful grazers and browsers—dairy cows in the wild. Thus, people are more

Buffalo at a Glance

Males (or bulls) weigh 1000–2000 pounds, are 5–6 feet tall at the shoulder hump, and are 9–11½ feet from nose to tail. Females (or cows) weigh 700–1000 pounds, are up to 5 feet tall at the shoulder, and measure 7–8 feet from nose to tail. Both sexes have short black horns that curve out and up and are pointed, with a head plus horn spread of up to 3 feet. Males have broader heads, wider horn spread, and less vertical rise. Female heads are narrower, more cowlike, and the horns look tall and slender. Buffalo have acute hearing and sense of smell, but only fair vision.

likely to make the mistake of approaching buffalo until they're so close the buffalo feels compelled to defend itself.

Keep Your Distance

Yellowstone Park has long required people to stay at least 75 feet away from buffalo, but park visitors often ignore this regulation. In thirty-five cases where rangers were able to measure the distance from which buffalo charged and injured people, the person was an average of 28½ feet away. Two people tried to pet or feed buffalo. Two people threw rocks or sticks at buffalo in a misguided—you might say demented—attempt to move the animals into better position for a photograph. In ten cases, people got within 50 feet of buffalo to pose for photographs. In 1983, a French man approached to within 6 feet of a bull buffalo to have his photograph taken by friends. The buffalo charged and tossed him 10 feet into the air. He died from his injuries. A total of eleven people have been tossed in the air for distances up to 15 feet. One of these people landed on the buffalo's back and was gored a second time when the buffalo twisted its head back and nailed him. Six people were within 10 feet of buffalo when they were charged. The moral of the story here is crystal clear—keep your distance from buffalo.

BEWARE OF BULLS
Bull buffalo are responsible for over 90 percent of all injuries to humans by buffalo.

Most of these incidents occurred along roads or in developed areas. They're classic examples of tourists behaving badly. But bull buffalo will go out of their way to displace hikers in the backcountry. Cross-country skiers in Yellowstone's backcountry routinely encounter buffalo. Free-ranging buffalo are a legitimate concern for people who venture into the backcountry of some parks and reserves, and for anybody tempted to try for a photograph of a buffalo beside a road.

HIKERS BEWARE: KING OF THE RANGE
Retired Yellowstone National Park Ph.D. biologist Mary Meagher, who specialized in buffalo throughout her long career, notes that bull buffalo often have a dominating, "King of the Range" mentality. If you stop 200 yards away from a group of four bulls, you certainly don't pose a threat to them, but there's a possibility that one bull will deliberately approach you. It's King of the Range and he's headed your way to show you who's boss. Don't wait until the bull is 25 yards away. Leave. Walk away the instant you realize the bull is moving toward you.

You Should Fear the Unknown

If you make the decision to get close to a placid-appearing buffalo chewing its cud at two in the afternoon, you can't possibly know what sort of interactions it's had with people or rivals the past few hours. Maybe someone tossed rocks at it. Perhaps it's a wounded bull that lost a mating battle with another bull. It's possible that someone yelled at it and stamped their feet in an effort to make the buffalo stand up for a photo. Incidents like this stress buffalo and have a cumulative effect; your approach could be the proverbial straw that breaks the camel's back.

Buffalo Behavior

During the mating season, bulls can be quite demonstrative. They vigorously roll in wallows. (Their hump prevents them from rolling all the way over.) They shake their heads and horns. They butt trees. They bellow; it sounds like someone is trying to take a bone away from a 2000-pound dog. They snort and paw. Are you likely to see any of these behaviors before a buffalo charges you? No. They're not likely to warn you away like a domesticated bull in a cartoon. But if you do notice any of these behaviors, pay heed and move away from the buffalo.

Seasonal issues. In some places, mating season starts in mid-June and extends until September. This is a bad time to test the patience of bulls. During the winter, buffalo operating on low energy reserves can be intolerant of intruders. That's more than half the calendar year.

Bull or Cow?

Most people encountering buffalo have no idea whether they're looking at bulls or cows. Size alone is not a reliable indicator. Young bulls and mature cows are about the same size. Bulls tend to have broader foreheads. The male anatomy of a bull standing on all fours is readily apparent. If you spot a lone buffalo or an isolated group of six or fewer, you're probably looking at bulls. Cow herds, however, are not composed exclusively of cows. There are always young bulls in the herd, and typically at least one mature bull.

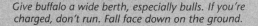

Give buffalo a wide berth, especially bulls. If you're charged, don't run. Fall face down on the ground.

What to Watch For

If you were to approach a cow herd, the first sign of anxiety you might notice would be simply that some animals stop feeding or whatever they were doing and stare at you. You'd see general uneasiness: Resting animals that get up and urinate or defecate. More staring in your direction. Heads up and tipped back a little while sniffing to scent you. It's all fairly subtle, but if you're close enough to prompt this kind of reaction, you'd better be paying attention enough to realize that you're making the buffalo uncomfortable. Rather than pushing forward, move away.

The Final Signal

A buffalo's tail position can be an accurate indicator of its mood. (Incidentally, a buffalo's tail is 12–18 inches long with a thick tuft of hair on the end. Native Americans removed the tendons and meat and made fly swatters from buffalo tails.) When a buffalo's tail is hanging straight down and switching, the animal is relaxed. If that tail goes straight out, the buffalo is getting nervous. When a buffalo's tail goes straight up, there's a distinct possibility it will charge. But a buffalo's tail also goes almost straight up when it's about to defecate, and buffalo have been known to charge without any overt behavioral warning. One second a cow and her calf are grazing with no apparent concern about your presence, the next second the cow is thundering toward you.

AVOIDING CONFRONTATIONS

Avoiding trouble with buffalo is easy: Keep your distance. Don't crowd them. Don't approach them for photographs.

Longtime Yellowstone ranger Rick McAdam, an avid runner, occasionally encounters buffalo while he's running on roads in the park. If a herd of buffalo is grazing 30 yards away from the east side of the road, McAdam takes the common-sense precaution of moving to the west side of the road. This increases his distance from the buffalo and makes him less threatening. In addition, buffalo slip and slide on concrete and asphalt. They don't like walking on paved roads or sidewalks.

If you're hiking in the backcountry and a lone bull or a cow herd with sixty animals is blocking your preferred travel route, detour around them. Theodore Roosevelt National Park recommends that people on foot or horseback stay 100 yards away from buffalo. That much distance is probably overkill, but it doesn't hurt to be prudent. On the other hand, it *will* be painful if you're stomped, gored, or butted by a buffalo.

IF YOU ARE CHARGED

No park or game refuge with buffalo offers any advice on what to do if you're charged. Most people panic and run. Some people have had the presence of mind to zigzag as they frantically ran away. Others tried to duck behind boulders or large trees. Some folks got away, some didn't. Mary Meagher says running from a charging buffalo is a serious mistake. If you run, the buffalo is likely to give chase. Buffalo are herbivores, not carnivores, so they're not chasing you like a cat after a mouse; it's a matter of dominance and personal space. Buffalo can turn on a dime; trying to dodge behind a boulder or tree isn't likely to help you avoid an aroused buffalo for long.

If you're charged at close range, Meagher recommends that you fall face down on the ground. Lie as flat as you can. Anatomically, it's difficult for a running buffalo to get its head down low enough to hook you. If you're lucky, the buffalo will run right by you without making contact.

Runners usually get hooked from behind and knocked down. After knocking people to the ground, buffalo generally move a short distance away and begin grazing. In a few instances, buffalo stood over people for several minutes. One person who tried to get up was promptly head-butted back to the ground, while another person who lay still was gored several times. The key to safety is to avoid being charged in the first place.

Where the Buffalo Roam

Badlands National Park, South Dakota
Custer State Park, South Dakota
Delta Junction, Alaska
Fort Niobrara National Wildlife Refuge, Nebraska
National Bison Range, Montana
Theodore Roosevelt National Park, North Dakota
Wichita Mountains National Wildlife Refuge, Oklahoma
Wind Cave National Park, South Dakota
Woods Buffalo National Park, Alberta/Northwest
   Territories
Yellowstone National Park, Wyoming

CHAPTER 3

Cougars

IMAGINE THIS:
You're walking along an old logging road out West with your seven-year-old son when you notice a cougar crouched just 60 feet off the side of the road. Surprised, you stare at the cougar. It stares back at you intently with its tail twitching. What should you do?

Documented Cougar Attacks
In the United States, 1890–1980: 12
In the United States and Canada, 1981–90: 20
In the United States and Canada, 1991–99: 53

You could spend a lifetime outdoors in cougar country without seeing one, let alone having a confrontation—but cougars occasionally prey on people. They stalk and ambush humans, just as they would a deer or elk. Of fifty-three attacks in the 1990s, twenty-one people never knew what hit them, or didn't see the cougar until it was too late to react. Nineteen children were injured in the 1990s. Sixteen of those children were in a group of people with adults and teenagers; it appears that cougars "select" small children as prey. More than half of all humans attacked by cougars have been less than four feet tall.

Cougars at a Glance

Males are 125–140 pounds, 2–3 feet tall at the shoulder, and about 7 feet long, including a 27–38 inch dark-tipped tail. Females are about one-third smaller: 100 pounds and 6 feet long. Cougars can run up to 45 miles per hour and are excellent tree climbers. Deer and elk are the mainstays of the cougar diet. Cougars are also called mountain lions or pumas.

Children are often the victims of cougar attacks. Have a response plan before going afield with kids.

WHERE ARE THE COUGARS?

Some parks and places where there have been cougar attacks post warning signs at trailheads, but the fact is, you could encounter a cougar almost anywhere in their range across Canada, Mexico, and the United States. Cougars have attacked people in the suburbs, in wildlands adjacent to metropolitan areas, and on wilderness lands. Many attacks occur on trails and lightly used roads—a logging road or Forest Service road that doesn't see a lot of traffic.

Cougar Activity Patterns

Cougars tend to be most active during the night and at dawn and dusk; however, this does not preclude a cougar being out at midday. A number of attacks have occurred in broad daylight, which is not surprising—that's when most people are out and about. If cougars were more active during the day, there would probably be more cougar predation on people.

Cougar Hunting Techniques

Cougars silently stalk and ambush their prey. They typically finish with a short sprint, leaping on their prey from behind. They kill deer with a bite to the neck at the base of the skull. To kill elk, cougars reach around the neck with their front leg, and pull back so forcefully they break the elk's neck.

AVOIDING TROUBLE WITH COUGARS

If you see a cougar, don't approach it. Limit your outdoor activities at dawn and dusk. Avoid cougar kill: Cougars will cover a kill with dirt and debris and return to feed; be alert for birds and other scavengers that might tip you off to a carcass and avoid dead animals in general.

Travel in a group, not solo. In particular, running or jogging in cougar country is a bad idea. Of eight adults attacked by cougars in Colorado, five were running (and one was riding a mountain bike). Hiking, walking, running, or bicycling with a group of adults is safer because you're less likely to be attacked, and you're more likely to survive because your companions can usually drive the cougar away and provide assistance. Have an adult at the front and rear of the group. (But see "Safety in numbers?," on page 37, for a cautionary note about hiking with mixed groups of children and adults.)

Pepper Spray and Cougars. People assume that since pepper spray usually "works" on bears, it will work on cougars. Be aware that pepper spray has not been tested on cougars. In contrast, pepper spray was tested on bears under laboratory conditions long before it was sold to the public. Inventor Bill Pounds and biologist Chuck Jonkel wanted to make sure that spraying a bear didn't just further irritate it. Thus far, zookeepers have used pepper spray effectively on tigers, African lions, and jaguars. Pepper spray could prove to be an outstanding defensive weapon for people being stalked or followed by a cougar.

Walking sticks. Many hikers carry a walking stick; it could be used to wallop a cougar.

Dogs and cougars. Aside from packs of well-trained lion-hunting hounds, dogs have little or no value as a deterrent when you're in cougar country. To the contrary, dogs have been involved in a significant number of aggressive lion-human incidents. This is true for small dogs and large dogs. Cougars routinely kill and eat dogs. They've been known to come into backyards and attack dogs in open-topped kennels. Biologists have documented cases where a dog off leash has tangled with a cougar and led it back to its owner.

KIDS AND COUGARS: PRETRIP PLANNING

Have a plan of action. Parents with kids and adults supervising children need to have a plan of action for cougar encounters or confrontations. Discuss plans with children before going afield. In the event of an encounter, this will help everyone take the correct actions instead of panicking and making the wrong moves.

Safety in numbers? Be aware that groups of people don't seem to deter cougar attacks on children. A cougar will watch and wait for an opportunity to grab a child that strays from the group. Children only a very short distance from a group of people have been attacked and adults were powerless to stop the cougar's initial move. Often, they didn't see anything and weren't aware of the situation until they heard a child screaming. It's best to keep kids within reach. Easier said than done, right? At the very least, keep kids in sight. Groups of small children (age ten and under) should be closely supervised by an adult.

CLOSE ENCOUNTERS: WHAT TO DO

If a cougar more than 50 yards away is watching you, or is following at set distance:

Don't run. This is especially important for kids. Flight might trigger pursuit.

Face the cougar. Don't turn your back on a cougar. Stand up.

Maintain eye contact with the cougar. Cougars prefer to ambush prey from behind. If the cougar knows you've seen it, an attack is less likely.

Adults: Pick up the kids. Given that children tend to frighten easily, adults should pick them up to prevent them from running or making sudden movements.

Another alternative is to instruct kids to grab your leg and hang on. At the very least, children should crowd around an adult. When you pick up children, or when they latch on to you or crowd around you, they don't look like prey.

Children: Don't move if you are closest to the cougar. If there's a group of children scattered around an adult, the children behind the adult should move toward him or her; if there's a *child between an adult and the cougar*, the adult should move toward the child.

Ready any weapon you're carrying, or pick up rocks and sticks in an aggressive, demonstrative manner.

If a cougar is within 50 yards and is intensely staring and making an effort to hide or conceal itself:

Do all of the above.

Make yourself look bigger. Raise your hands overhead. If you've got a jacket or a pack hold it up so you look even bigger and bulkier.

Attempt to move to safety. Don't run, but if there's a safer location (a building or car) available nearby, move toward it slowly while facing and watching the cougar. Try to get on higher ground than the cougar.

If a cougar is staring intensely and trying to hide, combined with crouching and/or creeping toward you:

Do all of the above.

Throw things at the cougar if it's close enough.

Smile. Show the cougar your teeth. To the cougar, you're displaying weapons.

Yell, shout, and make intimidating sounds. Your goal is to convince the cougar that you are not prey, and may in fact be dangerous.

If a cougar is staring intensely, with its tail twitching, body low to the ground/crouching, and ears erect, the cougar is waiting for a chance to attack. If the cougar's rear legs are also pumping or moving up and down and its ears are turned fur side forward, an attack is imminent:

Do all of the above.

Launch a preemptive strike by taking aggressive action toward the cougar.

If you have a weapon, use it. If you have a tree branch or walking stick, quickly run toward the cougar and shove the stick in its face. If you don't have a stick, yell and run toward the cougar with your hands overhead—but stop before you're within reach of its paws.

If a cougar attacks and makes contact:

Fight for your life. Use any weapon available: camera, binoculars, a knife, a fishing pole, or your fists. Direct your blows to the cougar's eyes, nose, ears, and face.

If a cougar attacks a child, adults should attempt to fight the cougar off by any means possible, including bare hands. It has worked, and the cougar rarely turns on its assailant.

If a cougar attacks and injures a child, then retreats a short distance after being driven off, guard the child and watch the cougar carefully—cougars have been known to return again and again, focused entirely on the child. One cougar ran between the legs of an adult who was trying to protect an injured child. Don't leave the child alone for an instant.

CHAPTER 4

Coyotes

> **IMAGINE THIS:**
> On millions of acres of Bureau of Land Management and U.S. Forest Service land out West, you can camp almost anywhere with just a few restrictions, but you've heard about coyotes attacking people. You vaguely remember a story about several coyote attacks on children in a park. Should you be concerned about coyotes?

The coyote, God's Dog, is one of the most persecuted mammals in North America. People shoot coyotes for sport. Professional government hunters gun down coyotes from helicopters on behalf of the livestock industry. We poison coyotes. We trap them. To no avail. Coyotes are thriving. Their numbers are increasing, and they're expanding their range. However, coyotes are usually wary of people and more inclined to avoid us than to attack us.

THE DANGER ZONE: POPULATED PLACES

Prior to 1981, there were few documented coyote attacks on people. From 1988 to 1997, coyotes injured twenty-one people in Southern California alone. Nationwide, fifty-six coyote-related human safety incidents were reported to the U.S. Department of Agriculture in 1990.

Many attacks have been on children under the age of five. In 1995, a coyote injured a fifteen-month-old girl in Griffith Park, located in the maw of Los Angeles. In 1996, a coyote attacked a three-year-old boy at the Windy Hills Open Space Preserve near Los Altos, California. In 1997, a coyote injured a twenty-two-month-old toddler in Tucson, at Arizona's Wildlife

Ridge Park. One day later, a coyote bit, but did not break the skin, of a two-year-old boy.

Fact

An estimated 5000 coyotes live in the city of Los Angeles.

The vast majority of coyote attacks on humans occur in areas where coyotes have become habituated to people and have received food from people. For this reason, coyotes in the suburbs are more dangerous than coyotes on remote public land. Coyotes residing in city parks or the "open spaces" adjacent to communities pose more of a threat than coyotes in large national parks. As a rule, coyotes in the wild are not a threat to humans. They avoid us, and wisely so.

One possible exception to this rule occurred in January of 1990 in Yellowstone National Park when a coyote charged a cross-country skier, knocked the man down, and bit him repeatedly. But this incident took place on a ski trail near Old Faithful, which is home to hundreds of employees and over-run by hundreds of snowmobilers every day—there's a good possibility the coyote was habituated to people and food-conditioned.

Habituated Coyotes

In some places, especially parks, coyotes have become accus-tomed to people, but they have not learned to associate people with food. These coyotes will tolerate humans in fairly close proximity, but they're not necessarily dangerous. If you're walking along a trail and a coyote notices you but goes back to its business instead of running away, there's no cause for alarm. The coyote is probably just used to people. So long as it doesn't approach you, there's nothing to worry about.

Coyotes at a Glance

Coyotes look like a small German shepherd with a shorter, bushier, black-tipped tail and a longer, narrower muzzle. The tail is carried low. They weigh 20–40 pounds, averaging 25 pounds. They are 4 feet long, including a foot-long tail, and are 20–24 inches tall at the shoulder. Coyotes can run up to 40 miles per hour. They are most active at dawn, dusk, and during the night, but can be seen any time of day.

Coyotes that have been fed by people and are accustomed to humans can pose a risk to toddlers and children.

WHEN TO BE WARY AND WHAT TO DO

You should be concerned if a coyote is aware of you and deliberately approaches you. If you're approached by a coyote at a picnic area in a park, or in a developed campground in a park or forest, there's a chance the coyote has been fed by people. This is the rare coyote that might attempt to snatch a child. Round up your kids. Be aggressive toward the coyote. Yell, stamp your feet, and throw rocks or sticks at it.

CHAPTER 5

Grizzly Bears

IMAGINE THIS:
You're hiking on a trail with your husband and two children
when you spot a grizzly feeding on a hillside about 125 yards
away. There's a stiff breeze blowing from the bear toward you,
and the bear does not appear to be aware of you. Now what?

ESSENTIAL GRIZZLY BEHAVIOR AND BIOLOGY
Personal Space, Territory, and Home Range

The key to understanding grizzly bear behavior is understanding how grizzlies defend their personal space. Personal space
is the area that, if entered, will cause an animal to fight or flee.
Grizzlies evolved in open country like Alaska's treeless tundra
or eastern Montana's prairies. Centuries ago, a female grizzly
with cubs had to contend with wolves, the North American
saber-toothed lion, and other grizzlies. When threatened, her
cubs couldn't climb trees. Often there was no cover where they
could hide. Thus, the best defense for a female with cubs was
a good offense. When forced by an intruder to make a quick
decision—fight or flee—grizzlies will sometimes charge their
assailant.

Figure a grizzly will react to your presence at a distance of
about 100 yards—the length of a football field. The majority
of injuries occur when the grizzly isn't aware of people until
they're within 60 yards or less. The closer you are when the
bear first becomes aware of you, the greater the risk it will
charge rather than retreat.

It's often said that grizzlies will defend their territory;
however, grizzly bears are not territorial. Territorial animals
defend an exclusive area. Wolf pack A won't allow wolf pack

B or C into its territory, and vice versa. Grizzlies don't defend an exclusive territory; rather, they have overlapping home ranges. Often, home ranges overlap at rich food sources like a berry patch or a spawning stream for salmon. Grizzlies don't defend their home ranges from other bears, let alone from people.

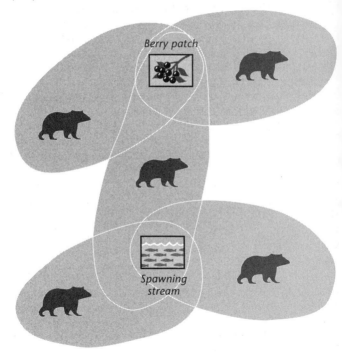

A grizzly lives in a home range that overlaps the home ranges of other bears. Grizzlies don't defend their home range from other bears—or people.

Grizzlies at a Glance

The Rocky Mountain male weighs 350–500 pounds, is 6–7 feet long, and about 36 inches at the shoulder. It can attain speeds of 35–40 miles per hour. Adults are not good tree climbers, but they are capable of "laddering" up the right tree. Grizzly hearing, vision, and smell are about the same as black bears, which is to say acute. Grizzly vision has not been clinically tested, but they have better eyesight than is commonly believed. Although they may be a tad nearsighted, they key on movement and pick out unusual shapes at considerable distances. They also have good peripheral vision. They notice silhouettes on ridge lines and bright colors. And grizzlies can see just fine at night.

Habituated Grizzlies

In response to a recurring stimulus with no rewards or punishment, a grizzly will begin to ignore the stimulus. If there's an abundance of natural food near a popular trail, grizzlies might learn to ignore hikers on that trail. There's a truce of sorts, provided hikers don't "reward" the bears by feeding them, or "punish" the bears by harassing them. Just remember that habituated grizzlies are not tame. They are not harmless.

Food-Conditioned Grizzlies

If a grizzly obtains food at a backcountry campsite or a developed campground just once, it will probably return for more. Once bears (black bears included) obtain food at a certain place, they'll put up with a lot of punishment for another food reward, and they'll often be more willing to tolerate people nearby. Food conditioning combined with habituation greatly increases the risk of conflicts and confrontations with people. Food-conditioned, habituated grizzlies have a history of killing and eating people.

SAFE RECREATION IN GRIZZLY COUNTRY

Avoidance is your number one, most critical tool for safely enjoying grizzly country. It emphasizes taking proactive measures to minimize your risk of encountering a grizzly. There are two keys to avoidance. One, don't attract grizzlies. Keep bears out of camp with careful consideration of campsite location and proper food storage. Two, keep a safe distance away from bears by being a defensive hiker.

Your Camp

Selecting a camp. Before starting out, ask land managers if people have had problems with grizzlies in the area where you plan on camping and hiking. Find out if you need to be aware of seasonal foraging areas—berry patches, spawning-fish streams—and avoid camping in those places.

When you first arrive in camp, inspect the area for signs of grizzly activity. If you find scat, check for undigested bits of plastic or trash. This would indicate there's a food-conditioned bear in the area, so you'd want to camp elsewhere. Look for evidence of digging. Check the fire ring for garbage. If you think the previous campers were lax on food handling or that a grizzly has been visiting the campsite because it found food and garbage left by previous campers, consider moving to a different campsite.

Travel corridors. Grizzlies, like black bears, generally choose the path of least resistance: trails, roads, ridge lines, addles, and natural travel corridors. Backpackers should not camp or store food in these areas.

Let grizzlies use their senses. Avoid windy areas. The wind might blow your scent away from grizzlies. Stay away from noisy places so that grizzlies can hear you: waterfalls, rushing streams and rivers, waves breaking on a lakeshore.

Grizzlies are curious. If your tent sticks out like a sore thumb due to shape, color, or location, a curious bear might decide to check it out. Bears investigate anything novel; a bright blue tent is more noticeable than an earth-toned tent. A rectangular tent sticks out more in a natural landscape than a dome. Try to visualize your camp from the perspective of a grizzly walking by at a distance of 50 or 100 yards. You don't want to stand out, you want to blend in.

Camp design. At the very least, your cooking/food storage areas should be 100 yards from your tent and sleeping area. The cooking/food storage areas should also be downwind of the sleeping area. Remember that cold air flows downhill at night.

Unexpected attractants. Human urine/excrement attracts grizzlies. Attend to your business well away from camp. At night, keep a conspicuously labeled NOT FOR DRINKING "pee bottle" in your tent to help you avoid the temptation of stepping a few feet out the door and relieving yourself. Don't spit sweet-smelling toothpaste on the ground. Grizzlies are also attracted to petroleum products; be careful not to spill fuel for stoves and lanterns. Store fuel, stoves, and lanterns with food and garbage.

Food Storage and Preparation

Storage. First, be aware of local regulations and accommodations for storing food. Food storage lockers and hanging poles are provided in some areas. Several parks now require the use of bear-resistant food containers (BRFC) in the backcountry. Whenever possible, use BRFCs for storing food.

If you don't have a BRFC, use a tree branch to hang food at least 10 feet off the ground and 4 feet from the tree's trunk. (The counterbalance method of hanging food is fully described in chapter 1, Black Bear.) No trees? Take food at least 100 yards away from camp and hope it's still there in the morning.

Cook where you can see. Cook in a spot that provides you with good visibility so you can see grizzlies approaching. Pay attention to wind direction; grizzlies are more likely to approach from downwind. It's prudent to keep pepper spray handy at your cooking site (see the discussion of pepper spray on page 55).

On the Trail
Hike in a group. As a general rule, the larger the group, the safer you are. Four or more hikers in a group is a good rule. Grizzlies are less likely to charge a group of people than an individual. This is why it's also important for the group to stick close together. There's a natural tendency to get widely spaced apart when you're on the move. If one person gets way ahead of the group and encounters a grizzly, the advantage of hiking in a group is lost.

Adults lead. In grizzly country, it's especially important to have an adult (or two) at the head of the line; that's the person most likely to be charged during a surprise encounter.

Pay attention. Your goal is to be aware of grizzlies before they're aware of you. Far too many hikers watch their feet and fail to pay attention to their surroundings. They'd walk right past a rhinoceros. Bring binoculars and use them frequently to sweep the country ahead of you. While you're stopped, listen for squirrels or birds scolding a bear. Smell the flowers . . . or perhaps a ripe carcass claimed by a grizzly.

Make noise when appropriate. For example, clap your hands and holler when visibility is limited. Make noise when there's a blind corner on a trail, in thick underbrush, or when you're about to crest a ridge and you can't see what's on the other side.

Bear Bells

For decades, hikers in grizzly country have attached bear bells to their packs or shoes, the idea being that the noise from the bells will alert bears to the presence of people and prevent a surprise encounter. Don't count on it. Bear bells aren't very loud. They can't be heard above the roar of a fast-moving stream or under other natural conditions. Bears in remote locations that have little exposure to humans don't pay much attention to the bells and they don't associate ringing bells with people. Bear bells are most effective on popular trails where bears have learned to associate people with ringing bells. Even so, not all bears in those areas will necessarily make the association.

Photographers: Don't Play Russian Roulette with Grizzlies

Photographers who approach grizzly bears—males, females with cubs, *any* grizzly—are playing Russian roulette. There's no way a photographer approaching a grizzly can possibly know when the invisible line will be crossed that puts the photographer inside the bear's personal space and forces the animal to make a decision: fight or flee? Once a photographer enters a grizzly's personal space, there are all sorts of variables that influence whether the bear will fight or flee. There's no way a photographer can predict what the bear will do.

Trail Running

Trail running in grizzly country is just asking for trouble. The issue for trail runners is not that a grizzly will see them running and give chase like a cat after a mouse; the issue is that runner will startle a nearby bear and then get charged. Trail runners routinely violate the principal safety guidelines for hikers: Be alert and pay attention to your surroundings, travel in a group of four or more, make noise when appropriate.

GRIZZLY ATTACKS DEMYSTIFIED

On rare occasions, grizzly bears prey on people. These incidents tend to occur at night. Grizzlies have gone into tents after people.

However, most grizzly bear attacks are actually defensive in nature. A hiker suddenly encroaches on the personal space of a nearby grizzly. The grizzly feels threatened. Fight or flee. It charges. When the hiker is no longer a threat—generally a minute or less—the grizzly leaves. The presence of cubs or a carcass probably increases the amount of personal space a grizzly requires, and increases the likelihood that the grizzly will charge when you encroach on that personal space.

There have only been a handful of cases where a bear that killed a person during a defensive encounter then began scavenging the body.

Menstruating Women and Grizzlies

There's no credible scientific evidence that menstrual odors are more attractive to bears than any other odor. There's no statistical correlation between bear attacks and menstruation.

The menstrual myth began one night in 1967 when a grizzly bear killed a menstruating woman in Glacier National Park—a woman wearing mosquito repellent, cosmetics, and clothing saturated with food odors. The bear was habituated to people and food-conditioned. That's what brought the bear and the woman into close proximity. What triggered the attack? Was it the odor of mosquito repellent? Menstrual blood? Or something else? Nobody knows.

We do know that the National Park Service, Forest Service, and other agencies hire women to work as rangers, fire lookouts, and trail crew members in the backcountry. Since that's not a problem, it's perplexing that one park still cautions menstruating women about venturing into bear country.

Sanitary Products: Common Sense Precautions

Use internal tampons rather than external pads.

Use unscented products, including tampons and cleaning towelettes.

Store used towelettes, pads, or tampons as carefully as you store food or garbage. It's a good idea to place them in a resealable plastic bag; a small amount of baking soda in the disposal bag will help absorb odor.

Burning tampons in a campfire is possible, but not practical. It takes a really hot fire and a considerable amount of time. Charred remains must be removed and stored with other garbage. Finally, burning tampons or garbage puts out odors that might attract grizzlies.

DO NOT bury tampons or pads. Bears of all types (or other creatures) are likely to smell them and dig them out.

Research on Menstrual Odors and Bears

A 1983 study *did* suggest that polar bears are attracted to odors associated with menstrual blood; however, the methodology of the study has been roundly criticized. Among other problems, the researcher gave polar bears a choice between used tampons with menstrual blood and plain paper toweling that held 5 milliliters or less of chicken, seafood, and other attractants. The polar bears had a preference for used tampons, but the fluid in a tampon has a powerful odor when it makes contact with air and starts to decompose. Black bear researchers now place lard in tampons because they hold the scent and are effective at luring animals to time-lapse cameras and live traps. The polar bears might have preferred chicken over menstrual blood had it been fermenting in a tampon, but only menstrual blood was tested.

Human Sexual Activity and Bears

There's not a shred of evidence that human sexual activity attracts bears. This is another myth that began in Glacier National Park. On a warm summer night in 1980, a grizzly killed and partially consumed a young man and a young woman camped near an illegal dump. Biologist and bear attack expert Stephen Herrero, who served on the board of inquiry investigating the deaths, has written, "The bear might have approached the teenagers because of the odors from sexual intercourse, but whether this was the case and what happened next are conjecture."

Conjecture, yet Glacier National Park's current bear literature says, "Although evidence is inconclusive, sexual activity or a woman's menstrual period may attract bears."

In popular literature, the statement "human sexual activity attracts bears" has been repeated so often that it's regarded as a fact. It's not a fact; it's an unsubstantiated theory based on conjecture.

Never Get Between a Sow and Her Cubs

The issue isn't getting *between* a sow and her cubs; the issue is getting close enough to encroach on the sow's personal space.

THE POWER AND PERILS OF PEPPER SPRAY

For biologist Chuck Jonkel, who did pioneering research on pepper spray, the number one rule for using pepper spray is: Don't put yourself in a situation where you need to use it. Instead of counting on pepper spray to get you out of trouble, use your brain to avoid confrontations with bears. In the words of Steve French at the Yellowstone Grizzly Foundation, pepper spray "ain't brains in a can."

You can't count on pepper spray to save the day. There have been a number of cases where people carrying pepper spray in a standard holster on their hip didn't notice a charging grizzly until it was too late to get to their pepper spray. The bear was on them before they could react.

Still, in national forests bordering Yellowstone Park, pepper spray has proven far more effective at stopping grizzlies than firearms. Most hunters carry firearms that are powerful enough to drop a bear, but they don't have the skills to deliver a fatal shot. Facing a charging grizzly is combat shooting; people tend to panic. Here are the pros and cons of pepper spray and firearms.

Pros:

Pepper spray works. Not always, but most of the time. Pepper spray usually deters bears from entering a camp and, yes, it has stopped charging grizzlies in their tracks.

Pepper spray is legal in national parks and other places where firearms are prohibited.

Pepper spray is far less expensive than a firearm, and really cheap insurance when you consider that forty bucks could save your life.

Pepper spray is nonlethal. In contrast, firearms kill or wound bears. During the past decade, elk hunters in the Yellowstone region have killed so many grizzlies in self-defense, there's a de facto grizzly bear hunting season.

Pepper spray has never made a bad situation worse by making a bear even angrier. Wounding a bear with a firearm does make a bad situation worse.

Pepper spray doesn't require much skill or practice. You don't have to contend with the recoil and muzzle blast of firearms. The spray spreads out in a cone shape like a shotgun blast. Almost anyone could "hit" a 55-gallon drum 30 feet away the first time they used pepper spray. Try that with a .357 magnum pistol, a 12-gauge shotgun with slugs, or a 30/06 rifle.

Pepper spray is relatively light (less than a pound) and can be carried on your hip in a handy holster, which leaves your hands free for doing chores around camp. Many people have had bears enter their camp; because pepper spray is convenient, you'll have it with you when you need it.

Pepper spray is safer for others. Spraying a bear in a developed campground would not pose a threat to other campers. Blazing away at a bear with a pistol or rifle would endanger other campers.

Cons:

Pepper spray is more prone to mechanical failures than firearms. You can always count on the first shot with firearms.

Crosswinds and headwinds greatly reduce the effective range of pepper spray. One pepper spray company advises people to spray a charging bear at a distance of 40 feet unless there's a headwind; then, you "may wish to wait until it is quite close before spraying." Right. It's highly unlikely that a person being charged by a grizzly would give any thought to wind direction. You'd yank off the safety clip and try to spray the bear. Imagine watching your cloud of pepper spray curve to the side in a crosswind before it hit the bear. Wind does not affect bullets at close range.

Rain knocks down pepper spray. Rain—sometimes hard rain—is common on the coast of Alaska, the coast of British Columbia, and other places with healthy bear populations. Rain does not affect bullets.

Most pepper spray holsters—and all safety clips— are clumsy affairs. The safety clips are klutzy and awkward to remove. Typical pepper spray holsters have a flap secured with Velcro that covers the spray cap and safety clip. It takes time to pull up the Velcro flap, grab the can of pepper spray, and remove the safety clip before pointing and spraying. One pepper spray company makes a hip holster that allows you to spray without removing the can, but it's more difficult to aim from your hip rather than to hold the can in front of you and instinctively point and spray. Plus, your hand and arm are at an unnatural angle while you're yanking the trigger mechanism as the grizzly rushes toward you. Firearms have fast, convenient safeties.

Cold weather adversely affects the performance of pepper spray. Carry pepper spray on your hip on a crisp fall morning when the temperature is 40 degrees and the effective range drops markedly. You have to sleep with your pepper spray when the temperature drops below freezing. In cold weather, you need to keep pepper spray inside of your jacket, so getting it out in an emergency is a slow process. Cold weather has no effect on properly maintained firearms.

Pepper Spray Guidelines

Buy spray approved by the Environmental Protection Agency.

The spray should be at least 225 grams/7.9 ounces.

The spray should have a minimum range of 25 feet.

Spray should be derived from oleoresin of capsicum, with a concentration of 1.4 to 2 percent capsaicin and related capsaicinoids.

Spray should fire a shotgun-cloud pattern, not a single stream.

Using Pepper Spray

It's a deterrent, not a repellent. Sometimes pepper spray is incorrectly described as a bear "repellent." It's not. It's a deterrent. Used properly—sprayed directly into a bear's face at close range—pepper spray is a highly effective deterrent. Don't use pepper spray like mosquito repellent and spray it on your tent, or around the perimeter of your camp. Bears are actually attracted to the residue of pepper spray.

Know your range. Under perfect conditions, pepper spray has a maximum range of 25–40 feet. Pace it off. If you don't, you might fire your pepper spray long before a bear is within range.

Practice, practice, practice. If you don't practice with pepper spray, you're likely to panic and be all thumbs when facing a bear, especially a charging grizzly. So practice. **Tip:** Some manufacturers sell inert cans for practice at about half-price. If you have outdated cans, they can also be used for practice.

Make your actions instinctive. You're most likely to use pepper spray under extremely stressful conditions, so all your actions have to be automatic.

✔ Carry your pepper spray in the same place—your left hip, your right hip, in a chest harness, etc.

✔ Practice opening the safety flap on the holster again and again and again.

✔ Practice removing the safety clip. Practice until you're confident you could have your can of pepper spray out of the holster and ready to fire without even thinking about it.

✔ If you plan on using a holster that allows you to spray without removing the can, practice with that rig, and that rig only. Practice removing the safety clip and reaching for the trigger. Shooting from the hip is not as instinctual as pointing the can at your target, so go to the expense of test-firing a can. You'll get four to six one-second blasts per can. Set up a target and practice. Can you hit what you're aiming at? Are you confident you could hit a bear charging toward you?

Testing. After you've test fired a can of pepper spray, wipe off all the residue as well as you can. The smell is attractive to bears, and during cold weather you're going to have the pepper spray inside your jacket and sleeping bag.

Pepper spray is not a toy. It's important to convince children that pepper spray is not a toy. When you test your spray, let kids go to the spot that was sprayed and touch some of the residue with the tips of their fingers. Then have them lick their fingertips. Hot! Note that milk is better than water for cooling your mouth.

An Unanswered Question

Many people sleep with pepper spray so that if a bear enters their tent at night they can spray it. Would you be incapacitated after spraying inside a tent? For how long? Remember, pepper spray doesn't always work. On occasion, it fails to deter a bear. Furthermore, bears that have been sprayed have sometimes returned in a manner of minutes. Keeping pepper spray in your tent could save your life, but there are no guarantees. It could backfire.

ENCOUNTERS WITH GRIZZLIES: WHAT TO DO

Most commonly, you will see a grizzly in the distance, unaware of you. Don't alert the bear. If it's blocking the trail, wait it out or keep tabs on the bear as you make a wide detour around it.

Surprise Encounters

Plan ahead. What will you do if a grizzly enters your camp at night? Plan ahead so you don't panic during a surprise encounter. This is especially important when you're camping with kids. Who responds with deterrents? Who stays with the children?

A charging grizzly. If you don't see a grizzly until it's charging toward you, stand your ground. Have kids trained to get right behind you and grab your leg so they don't run away; it's better to have them coming toward you than scattering in all directions. Ready your deterrent if you have time. Fire when the grizzly reaches 7–10 yards. If you can't get to your deterrent, just stand your ground. Don't play dead until the bear makes contact. There's a good chance the bear will stop short of making contact. If it stops, don't make any fast moves. Don't yell. Hold tight a few moments and see if the bear moves off. If it doesn't, try taking the slowest steps of your life and quarter (move at an angle) away from the bear. Keep an eye on the bear. Stop if your movement appears to agitate the bear.

Eye Contact

Staring at a bear or making direct eye contact is not likely to influence the outcome of an encounter or to affect the bear's behavior. During a standoff, you need to watch the bear so you know if it's approaching, standing still, or moving away.

You startle a grizzly 40 yards away. It rears up on its hind legs, then drops to the ground and moves about nervously. Don't run. Ready your deterrent, and pick a spot 7–10 yards away so you know when you're going to fire if the bear charges or approaches. Identify yourself as a human by calmly talking and slowly—not frantically—waving your arms overhead. If the bear is not moving toward you, carefully move away. Increase your distance. If the bear approaches, stand your ground. If it keeps coming, start waving your arms and yelling forcefully. If you're with a group of people, stand next to each other.

Climb a tree to escape a charging grizzly? If you don't see a grizzly until it's charging, it's probably too late for tree climbing. Grizzlies rarely charge unless they're startled at close range, and an aroused grizzly can cover 60 yards in three or four seconds. Even if you happened to be standing beneath a perfect climbing tree when you saw a grizzly charging, how high could you climb in four seconds?

If you're not standing beneath a tree, that means you'd have to run for a tree, and you're not supposed to run from bears. Running will just provide more motivation for the charging grizzly. Will you have time to run for a tree and climb 10 feet above ground before the bear arrives?

Playing dead. Never play dead if a bear enters your tent or dwelling at night. It doesn't matter if it's a grizzly bear or a black bear. Assume the bear is attempting to prey on you and fight back by any means available.

If a grizzly charges you and you don't have a weapon, or don't have time to get to your weapon, stand your ground until the bear makes contact, then play dead to convince the bear that you are not a threat. For years people have played dead by curling up in a ball, but there's a better way. Lie face down on your stomach with your elbows tucked tight against the side of your head and your hands locked together behind your head and neck. Sometimes bears flip people over; if this happens roll until you're on your stomach again. (This is fun to practice with kids.)

Try not to scream or yell. The less you struggle and move around, the sooner the grizzly will leave. Believe it or not, bears in these situations usually exercise considerable restraint. Like a full-grown female grizzly wrestling with her cub, they're holding back; they're not biting and clawing full force. But if you struggle and fight back, the bear will most likely intensify its efforts. After you think the bear has left, wait a while before lifting your head and looking around. Make sure the bear is gone. Sometimes bears will move a short distance away and watch to make sure you're really "dead." If you get to your feet while a nearby bear is watching, they'll return to finish the job.

WARNING

If a bear of any type keeps biting you for a pro-longed amount of time, or if you're convinced the bear is feeding on you, fight back. Never play dead if you suspect that a bear is preying on you.

CHAPTER 6

Javelinas

IMAGINE THIS:
You're walking up a deep, sandy wash in the Sonoran Desert when you catch a whiff of musky, almost skunky odor. You stop. You hear grunting. Curious, you walk around a bend and see a herd of nine javelina, including two babies. They turn to face you and stare in your direction. You notice the hackles on their backs rising, and the skunky odor gets much stronger. Suddenly the herd whirls and runs the other way.

Javelinas, also known as collared peccary, are tough desert dwellers with a fearsome reputation. "In the old days," wrote Theodore Roosevelt in 1893, "it had been no uncommon thing for a big band to attack entirely of their own accord, and keep a hunter up a tree for hours at a time." William T. Hornaday, turn-of-the-twentieth-century director of the New York Zoological Park, wrote that "An enraged peccary, athirst for blood, is to any one not armed with a rifle or first-rate spear a formidable antagonist." (Both are quoted in *Dangerous to Man,* by Roger Caras.)

JAVELINA SOCIAL LIFE
Despite tall tales of javelina herds numbering in the hundreds, there are typically 8–12 javelinas in a herd. An Arizona biologist who counted the number of javelinas in over 500 different herds never saw a herd of 40, and only 6 herds included more than 30 animals.

Within a herd, there are constant tussles over food and space. These disputes are settled with loud grunting and squealing and powerful head thrusts that bring into play straight tusks an inch or two long. Unlike those of warthogs, the tusks of javelinas don't visibly protrude. They're more like the canines on a dog or cat.

Javelinas at a Glance

Javelinas have long, piglike snouts and bristly, salt-and-pepper gray hair with a light collar over their necks and shoulders. They weigh 30–40 pounds, are 34–40 inches long, and stand 20–22 inches tall at the shoulder. They have poor vision but outstanding senses of smell and hearing. They run up to 25 miles per hour. When alarmed, javelinas raise their hackles and emit a strong musky smell from scent glands on their backs. You'll find javelinas in Arizona, New Mexico, and Texas.

Feeding javelinas or walking with dogs in javelina country increases the possibility of an encounter.

Coyotes and cougars prey on javelinas, particularly the young. To deter predators, the herd acts as a defensive unit, with mature javelinas protecting juveniles. They'll charge toward a predator. It's this protective instinct that occasionally leads to confrontations with people.

JAVELINA ATTACKS

Most "attacks" are really a case of confused javelinas running in the wrong direction. A herd of javelinas and a person accidentally find themselves in close quarters. If the person is downwind, the javelinas won't be able to identify the intruder by smell. They probably won't see the person because their vision is so poor. The instant one javelina panics and runs, the whole herd will follow. Should the herd run toward a person, it's easy to understand why it would seem like a charge or attack, but it's just a case of the javelinas trying to get away and not knowing which way to go.

Stories about javelina attacks in the wild are legion, but documented human injuries are rare. This is probably a combination of very few people being injured, and the injuries being minor. Of course, "minor" injuries is a relative term. The injuries might not be life threatening, but being gashed on the ankle or calf by a javelina would be a painful, frightening experience.

Backyard Encounters

The few human injuries from javelinas tend to result from conflicts in suburban and semirural areas. Pet dogs often enter into the equation. Green Valley, Arizona, seems to be a hot spot for this type of encounter. Green Valley is a retirement haven in the desert south of Tucson. Many homes are on an acre or several acres of land surrounded by prime javelina habitat.

Some residents deliberately feed javelinas. Others inadvertently attract javelinas with gardens, tasty flowers and plants, and watering systems for their yards. Late at night a dog needs to do its business. The dog's owner opens the back door and steps outside with the dog. There's a herd of javelinas in the backyard. They see the dog as a threat. They attack. The dog owner leaps into the fray and tries to protect the pooch. Both the dog and the dog's owner get injured.

If you choose to live in javelina country but don't want javelinas in your backyard, eliminate all attractants or fence your yard. If javelinas have obtained food or water on your property, you'll need a sturdy fence, because javelinas easily bash through the flimsy ones. Once they've established a travel route to food or water—the trails are obvious—javelinas are not easily deterred.

Dogs and Javelinas: A True Story

Dogs love to run free, so one day Michelle Brown, a biologist with the Nature Conservancy, took her three dogs for a walk on Bureau of Land Management land in Arizona, where it was perfectly legal and appropriate to let the dogs off the leash to roam at will. One of the dogs ran into a herd of about fifteen javelinas, including several babies. Naturally, the dog high-tailed it back to mom. Brown leaped up onto a large boulder and her dogs joined her while three javelinas, athirst for blood, tried to get at them. Brown had the dog's leashes in hand, so she swung them at the thoroughly agitated javelinas. After a minute, the javelinas ran off.

Theodore Roosevelt's comments aside, it's difficult to imagine javelinas behaving in this manner toward a lone human. Dogs change the dynamics of an encounter with javelinas. Javelinas no doubt regard dogs as coyotes—the enemy. As a result, avelinas will chase and injure dogs. Dog owners need to be aware of this before letting their pets run free in javelina country. The odds of having a confrontation are low, but it could happen. All dog owners need to assess the risk for themselves—and for their pets.

JAVELINA ENCOUNTERS IN THE WILD: WHAT TO DO

To avoid unwanted meetings with javelinas, be aware that the weather strongly influences where and when you'll find them. During strong winds, javelinas will feed on the leeward side of a hill or in canyon bottoms. When it's cold out, they feed on warm, sunny slopes. If it's hot, javelinas bed down in drainages or in deep brush that offers shade.

In the rare event that you have a close encounter with a herd of javelinas, remember that they don't see well. Talk or yell so they know where you are. This increases the likelihood that the javelinas will run away from you rather than accidentally charge toward you. If a herd does run toward you, try to get up a tree or hop up on a boulder large enough to get you out of reach. You won't have much time—javelinas are lightning quick. In addition, the odds of finding a handy tree or boulder in the desert are quite remote.

CHAPTER 7

Moose

IMAGINE THIS:
You're speeding down a hill on a groomed cross-country ski trail when you spot a cow moose feeding on willow buds about 5 yards off the trail at the bottom of the hill. What's the best course of action?

In Alaska, moose injure five to ten people a year—that's a higher yearly average than black bears and grizzlies combined. During the past decade, moose in Anchorage have killed two people. Moose might look ungainly—one observer remarked that they appear to have been made of spare parts from other animals—but they're big, strong, fast, and quick to defend themselves if they feel threatened.

AVOIDING CONFRONTATIONS

Don't approach moose. Like other animals, moose have an area around them that, if entered, will cause them to fight or flee. If a wolf, dog, bear, or human enters the "personal space" of a moose, it might charge.

Give cows with calves a wide berth. Cow moose are extremely protective of their calves. They'll defend their calves from a grizzly bear, so they won't hesitate to charge after you. If you see a calf, but no cow, be extremely careful—you may have gotten between them. Try to locate the cow and move away without drawing her attention. Be aware that the 200–400-pound calves can be dangerous by themselves. They're far less assertive than adult moose, but they are capable of injuring a predator—or you.

Moose at a Glance

Moose are dark brown and horse-sized. Shiras bull moose in the Lower 48 states weigh 800–1100 pounds. Cows weigh 600–800 pounds. They are 6 feet tall at the shoulder. Alaska bull moose weigh 1000–1600 pounds. Cows average 800–1200 pounds. Male antlers of both Shiras and Alaska moose are on average 4–5 feet wide. Moose can run 30–35 miles per hour. Their sense of smell is excellent, and their hearing is acute. Their vision is generally poor, but moose will notice movement at considerable distances.

This illustration shows the size of a typical male moose in relation to an average-sized man. In "real life," don't get anywhere near this close to a moose!

Don't feed the bears ... or the moose. Fed moose quickly habituate to people, then approach strangers expecting a snack and get angry when they aren't fed. In urban areas, these habituated moose have approached children on their way to school. In 1997, a six-year-old boy walking to school in Evanston, Wyoming, came within 10 feet of a cow moose and her calf. The cow butted the boy to the ground and kicked him with her front hooves.

Feeding moose encourages them to stay in populated areas where confrontations with people are more likely. Relatively few people get hurt by moose, but law enforcement officials are forced to kill far too many "aggressive" moose in the name of public safety.

Bad situations. During the fall mating season, bull moose are often in an agitated state. So are the cows. During the winter, moose are hungry. They get tired of walking through snow; this is not the time to test their temper. In spring, it's foolish to take chances with cow moose and their calves.

Dogs + Moose = Trouble. During Alaska's Iditarod sled dog race, moose have charged entire teams and their mushers. Moose treat dogs like their enemy, the wolf. Even in places where there haven't been wolves for generations, moose sometimes must contend with packs of feral or pet dogs. Moose calves are particularly vulnerable, which makes cow moose especially protective. If your dog starts barking at a moose or approaches a moose, the moose will defend itself by lunging and kicking at the dog, or by chasing it. A wolf would dodge the moose and stay out of reach; your dog will probably run straight back to you, bringing with it an infuriated moose.

Moose will go over or through fences to get into yards with barking dogs. They'll go out of their way to get at a dog on a leash. It's best not to hike or camp with dogs in moose country.

MOOSE ENCOUNTERS: WHAT TO DO

Moose behavior and body language can alert you to potentially dangerous situations. Your first sign that a moose is aware of your presence is often that it simply stops what it's doing and looks at you. It might stop feeding or walking and look your way. A moose bedded on the ground might get to its feet and stare in your direction. Its ears will probably swivel toward you. It's using sight and scent to determine what you are.

You can stay put, or move away from the moose. If it's in your travel route, detour around it in a manner that increases your distance from the moose. Before you move, take a look at the terrain and cover and make sure your movement won't make the moose feel like it's cornered.

Keep a watchful eye on the moose. If it lowers its head and ears and the hackles on its neck and back go up, you're the one who needs to start thinking about a good escape route. Moose also lick their lips when agitated. Back away. If you're too close, look for a tree to climb or a large object to get behind. Increase the distance between you and the moose in any way possible.

Fact

Moose can kick back with their hind legs like a horse, but more often they strike out with their front legs. This is a thousand pound animal with rock-hard hooves about 3 inches wide and 6 inches long. Ouch.

Cross-Country Skiers and Moose

Because cross-country skiers are often moving at a fast pace, there's a potential for suddenly coming upon a nearby moose.

If you're zooming down a hill and find yourself on a collision course with a moose at the bottom of the hill, sit down. Unless you're sure about your ability to maneuver around the moose, just sit down as far away as possible. If you land so close to the moose that being charged is a distinct possibility, quickly assess the situation. Can you get to your feet and ski away? If the snow is shallow enough, are you better off removing your skis so that you have more maneuverability?

Moose Along the Trail

Both hikers and cross-country skiers run the risk of encountering a moose along the trail. If the moose is bedded down or focused on eating and a safe distance away (at least 50 feet), it's generally safe to go by. If the moose is aware of you, watch for signs of agitation: lip licking, head lowered, ears back, hair standing up on the moose's back and neck. Back off and wait or, if you must continue, go way around the moose.

Charge!

If a moose charges, your best bet is to get up a tree. No tree? Run, or try to get behind a boulder or tree. If you're lucky, adrenaline will help you move quick enough to outmaneuver the moose. Sometimes moose will simply run off after knocking a person down. Other times, they stomp and kick with all four feet. Curl up in a ball and do your best to protect your head with your arms. Lie still. (Easier said than done.) Don't get up and try to move away until the moose has moved off a good distance or it may renew its attack.

If you think someone is about to be charged by a moose and you're a safe distance away, yell or make loud noise that might distract the moose. This might buy the victim enough time to get away.

CHAPTER 8

Wolves

IMAGINE THIS:
You're planning a family canoe trip to a remote lake in Canada, and you've heard that wolves in the area are almost tame. They'll approach people and campsites; they'll grab camera bags and loose gear and run off with it, just like playful puppies. Should you pack a video camera, or choose a different location?

KEY STATISTICS

After a wolf injured a boy in Alaska in 2000, biologist Mark McNay, with the Alaska Department of Fish and Game, gathered and reviewed reputable accounts of wolf–human encounters during which the wolves showed little fear of people. His research documented 80 incidents.

There were three clear-cut cases of attempted predation. All 3 involved children. Two cases involved "fearless" wolves. In 16 cases, wolves bit people or bit into their clothing. There were 6 severe bites; none were life threatening. Four of the 6 severe bites involved children; in every case, the children's injuries would have been more severe if adults hadn't intervened. Thirty-nine cases included "elements of aggression" by the wolves.

Nineteen incidents involved biologists. Biologists put themselves in situations an everyday hiker or camper would never experience. As McNay's report noted, "In February during a wolf capture attempt from a helicopter, a biologist darted an alpha female wolf. The animal was immobilized, but the capture team couldn't approach because the alpha male aggressively charged each time the helicopter set down."

Twelve cases involved wolves with rabies or suspected rabid wolves. Six cases involved people accompanied by dogs; wolves bit 2 people accompanied by dogs. Ten incidents involved people working on the Alaska pipeline in the 1970s; pipeline workers routinely fed wolves.

Wolves at a Glance

Males weigh 70–110 pounds; females weigh 60–80 pounds. Males are 6–6½ feet from tip of nose to end of tail; females are 4½–6 feet long. Shoulder height in both is 26–32 inches. Foot size is 4 inches wide by 5 inches long. Wolves can achieve speeds estimated at 35 miles per hour.

WOLVES AND PEOPLE: THE BIG PICTURE

The increase in the number and distribution of wolves in Minnesota during the past two decades has resulted in more wolves living near people than at any time in Minnesota's history. In addition, wolves may have less to fear of humans than they did three decades ago when they were heavily persecuted. The potential for a wolf harming a human is therefore higher.

—Ph.D. Biologist Steven H. Fritts,
in *The Wolves of Minnesota*

Although the potential for a wolf harming a human exists in today's world, actual cases of wolves injuring people usually involve habituated wolves or wolves interacting with a dog. In Minnesota's Superior National Forest, about nineteen million visitor days have been recorded without a single wolf attack. Throughout wolf country in Canada, Alaska, and the West, millions of safe visitor days are recorded in parks and wilderness areas. For a typical hiker or camper, the only wolf you need to be concerned about is a fearless, habituated wolf.

Dubious Information about Wolf Attacks

When a wolf attacked and injured a boy near Yakutat, Alaska, in April of 2000, an *Anchorage Daily News* article about the incident concluded by noting that, "in Canada, at least one person has been killed by wolves in the past 50 years. A 24-year-old woman was attacked by a pack of five at the Haliburton Forest and Wildlife Reserve in Ontario in 1996."

The wolves that killed the woman had lived their entire lives in captivity. When the attack occurred, they were living in a fifteen-acre enclosure. The woman had just started working, and had only been in the enclosure with the wolves twice before. Wolves can be dangerous to humans, but much of the wolf's ferocious reputation is based on exaggeration, distortion, and misinterpretations of wolf behavior.

Wolves and Dogs

In April of 2000, the Greenlee County Sheriff's Department in eastern Arizona got a radio call from a rancher who said he was being attacked by wolves. The rancher was at a remote cabin. He had six dogs with him. U.S. Fish and Wildlife spokesperson Vicki Fox told the *Eastern Arizona Courier*, "The wolves were focusing on the dogs . . . I believe the dogs fueled this situation. I believe the [wolf] pack saw it as an invasion of their territory. It's breeding season for the wolves."

March 1999. A woman walking her dog on a trail in Pacific Rim National Park in Canada encountered a wolf. She picked up her dog and headed back to her car. Two more wolves emerged. All three wolves followed at a distance of about 10 yards.

2002. A woman jogging with two Labrador retrievers in Gila Hot Springs, New Mexico, ran into a pair of wolves. The dogs ran toward the wolves, then returned to their owner. One wolf followed. "It didn't even see me. It was much more interested in the dogs." When the wolf got within 10 or 15 feet, the woman threw rocks at it and drove it away.

Territorial animals like wolves or nesting bald eagles defend an exclusive area from others of the same species. There's little or no overlap.

After a wolf killed a rancher's dog in Montana, Joe Fontaine of the U.S. Fish and Wildlife Service told the Associated Press that fourteen dogs had been killed by wolves in Montana since 1987. "Wolves are very territorial," said Fontaine. "They view dogs as another canine intruder in their territory."

There have been other cases where wolves that would not ordinarily approach people did so in order to interact with people's dogs. Although there's little chance you'll find yourself in close quarters with a wolf that's after your dog, keeping a dog in camp or walking a dog in wolf country does run up the risk of having an encounter.

Don't Feed Wolves

In 1999 and 2000, kayakers and campers at Vargas Island Provincial Park, British Columbia, not only fed wolves, they hand fed them. The wolves interacted with people; they'd crouch in front of people and then run in a little circle and return. These wolves would enter camps and grab shoes, clothing, and various camping gear. One night a wolf tugging on a camper's sleeping bag awakened the occupant. The man shouted at the wolf. The wolf attacked. Other campers drove the wolf away, but it took more than fifty stitches to close the man's wounds.

"Fearless" Wolves

In Ontario's Algonquin Provincial Park, there have been five incidents where wolves exhibited fearless behavior for weeks before biting people. The wolves entered camps and grabbed sleeping bags, tennis shoes, and other gear. They approached people. In one case, a wolf approached and jumped toward a woman four times. She thought it was more playful than aggressive. Earlier in the day, in the wee hours of the morning, the same wolf had bitten a twelve-year-old boy who was sleeping under the stars. Park officials did not regard this as an act of predation. Rather, they "speculated that the wolf's obsession with chewing and tearing human clothing and camping gear led to the wolf's pulling on an occupied sleeping bag" and injuring the boy inside.

These incidents occurred in the 1980s and 1990s. More recently, a memo from a Denali National Park bear management ranger said the Alaska park "has had its hands full with curious campground wolves over the last couple of seasons. They have carried away shoes and children's toys on a number of occasions."

If you hear about "fearless" or "habituated" wolves in a place you plan on camping, it would be prudent to go somewhere else.

Wolves and Kids

Of the six people who have been severely bitten by wolves, four were children. Two boys got nailed under similar circumstances. In each case, the boys didn't spot the wolf until it was about 10 yards away. They ran. The wolf chased them down.

Just as children shouldn't run from bears or cougars, they should not run from wolves.

AVOIDING TROUBLE WITH WOLVES

✔ Stay away from "fearless" or "habituated" wolves.
✔ Leave your dog at home.
✔ Don't work as a wolf biologist.

CHAPTER 9

Rabies

> **IMAGINE THIS:**
> *Your family is camped in a state park, and in the middle of the day you spot a raccoon walking along the road toward your campsite. You're no expert on raccoons, but this one seems a bit lethargic. As it walks toward your campsite, it weaves and totters like a drunk. What should you do?*

WHAT IS RABIES AND HOW DO PEOPLE GET IT?

Rabies is an infectious viral disease that affects the nervous system of humans and other mammals. You can't get rabies from snakes, birds, or fish. Rabies is not spread from contact with the blood, urine, or feces of a rabid animal; the rabies virus is spread through saliva. Typically, people get rabies from the bite of a rabid mammal. Getting bit by a rabid animal is not a death sentence—provided you get rabies shots. If you ignore a bite and give the rabies virus time to reach your central nervous system, then rabies is an incurable, 100 percent fatal disease.

In rare cases, rabies can be spread when saliva from a rabid animal contacts an open wound or mucus membranes—your mouth or nose. In other words, a friendly lick or kiss from a rabid dog could be the death of you. Bats, coyotes, fox, raccoons, and skunks are the wild mammals most commonly infected with rabies.

Rabies Cases in the United States

Humans	5
Raccoons	2778
Skunks	2223
Bats	1240
Foxes	453
Cats	249
Dogs	114

Source: "Rabies Surveillance in the United States During 2000," Centers for Disease Control and Prevention website, *www.cdc.org.*

Types of Rabies

There are two types of rabies. The most common form is known as paralytic or "dumb" rabies. The infected animal will act shy or timid. It may have paralysis of the lower jaw and muscles. It often rejects food. On the other hand, animals with "furious" rabies are hostile. They snap and bite at objects. They produce more saliva and look like they're foaming at the mouth. The word rabies is actually derived from a Latin word that means "to rage." These symptoms of dumb and furious rabies, however, are not always obvious.

Don't Let Rabies Sneak Up on You

In a way, rabies is sneaky. You get bit on the hand by a cute little raccoon you were feeding by hand at a campground. It didn't seem to be acting strange, it just nipped you. You don't want to get rabies shots, so you decide to wait and see if you develop any rabies symptoms. But early rabies symptoms are so mundane—headache, sore throat, fever, and generally feeling tired—you might ignore them, or fail to associate them with your raccoon bite. A month goes by and basically you're fine, right?

Wrong. All this time the rabies virus has been working toward your central nervous system. You can get shots to kill the rabies virus before it begins replicating in your brain, but once that happens, you're dead, and rabies shots won't do you a bit of good.

WARNING

If you get bit and you are unable to test the animal for rabies, or if the animal tests positive, get rabies shots.

Rabies: A Bad Way to Die

Once the noticeable symptoms of rabies arrive, you have about ten days to live. Victims develop hydrophobia—a fear of water due to throat spasms. Hallucinations are common. People drool a lot and suffer paralysis. The disease ends with a raging fever and total disorientation.

Alarming Fact

About 80 percent of the people who need rabies shots initiated contact with the animal that bit them. It wasn't a case of a rabid animal chasing after a person; the person went to the animal.

PREVENTING AND RECOGNIZING RABIES

Don't touch wild animals. Never attempt to feed a wild animal, especially campground beggars. Avoid contact with unfamiliar animals—stray dogs and cats are especially problematic because you don't know if they've had rabies vaccinations.

Don't try to rescue a sick animal. Call animal control or an animal rescue group. You should also call an animal control officer if you see a wild or domestic mammal acting strangely.

When camping out, sleep in a tent or enclosed structure, not on the ground under the stars.

Signs of Rabies in Animals

✔ Aggression
✔ Increased drooling
✔ Problems swallowing
✔ Wild animals moving slowly or acting tame
✔ Stumbling, wandering in circles, walking like a drunk
✔ Nocturnal animals out during the day
✔ General sickness: matted hair, sores, the tremors
✔ Changes in behavior: A friendly pet snaps at you or tries to bite you

A note of caution. You can't tell if an animal is rabid just by looking at it. Occasionally there's a legitimate reason for nocturnal skunks or raccoons to be out and about during the day. In some animals, the symptoms of rabies are almost indistinguishable from the symptoms of distemper. Still, if you notice any of these symptoms in an animal, and especially any combination of these symptoms, be cautious.

IF YOU'RE BITTEN BY A WILD ANIMAL

Wash your wound with soap and water for five minutes, and then treat it with a topical antibiotic if it's readily available. It's important to clean the wound soon after you've been bitten because the rabies virus perishes rapidly when exposed to detergents. See a doctor as soon as possible.

The only way an animal can be tested for rabies is to examine some of its brain tissue, so if you don't bring the animal that bit you into your local health department for testing, there's no way professionals can determine whether or not it had rabies—you'll be given rabies shots as a precaution. Thus, if you can safely capture or kill the animal that bit you, do so. Or call animal control for assistance with this task. Take the whole carcass to your local public health department. It's important to leave the head intact so the brain tissue can be tested.

You're Three Days from the Road—No Worries

Only 80 percent of the rabid animals that bite you will give you the disease. Even better, it usually takes twenty to sixty days for the rabies virus to reach a human's central nervous system; it depends on where you're bitten. A bite on the ankle or lower leg takes roughly sixty days; twenty days for a bite on your face. So even if you get bit by a skunk that you're sure has rabies when you're deep in the backcountry, there's no need to panic. Clean your wound properly and head for home promptly. Don't lollygag for a week, but don't worry about getting rabies in the next day or two. When you get out of the woods, get your rabies shots right away.

Rabies Shots

In the past, people who were bitten by a rabid animal, or an animal they suspected might have rabies, had good reason to dread getting rabies shots. You took twenty-six shots directly into the wall of the abdomen. It was painful. Today, your first injection is a human rabies immunoglobulin that provides immediate resistance to the rabies virus. It makes the body produce antibodies that kill the virus. It's administered at the site of the bite. A second rabies vaccine that helps the body build resistance to the virus is administered in your arm five times during the next four weeks. Six shots, that's it. Get the shots if you're the least bit suspicious about having been bit by a rabid mammal.

Selected References

CHAPTER 1. BLACK BEARS

Fair, Jeff. *The Great American Bear*. Minoqua, Wis.: NorthWord Press, 1990.

Herrero, Stephen, and Andrew Higgins. "Follow-Up Discussion with Stephen Herrero: Fatal Injuries Inflicted to People by Black Bear." In *Proceedings of the Fifth Western Black Bear Workshop*, 1993. Herrero is regarded as the world's top authority on bear attacks. For *accurate* data on bear attacks, read any of Herrero's published research or his classic book *Bear Attacks: Their Causes and Avoidance* (Guilford, Conn.: Lyons Press, revised edition 2002). Beware—there are a slew of bear-attack books on the market that have the same basic format: Man meets bear. Bear kills or injures man. Clinical descriptions of the injuries. Author's analysis of the accident. These books are filled with biased, inaccurate information.

CHAPTER 2. BUFFALO

Caslick, Jim, and Edna Caslick. "Bison–Human Incidents in Yellowstone, 1963–99. *The Buffalo Chip,* newsletter for National Park Service employees in Yellowstone (January–March, 2000).

Meagher, Mary. Telephone interview with the author. August 2002.

CHAPTER 3. COUGARS

Associated Press. "Wolf Attack Takes Family's Dog." *The Montana Standard,* April 2, 2002.

Beier, Paul. "Cougar Attacks on Humans in the United States and Canada." *Wildlife Society Bulletin* 19, no. 4 (1991): 403–12.

Colorado Division of Wildlife. *Mountain Biker Has Standoff with Mountain Lion.* Wildlife report, October 22, 1997.

Deurbrouck, Jo, and Dean Miller. *Cat Attacks: True Stories and Hard Lessons from Cougar Country*. Seattle: Sasquatch Books, 2001. Loaded with accurate statistics on cougar attacks. Excellent analysis of the simplistic theory that more sport hunting of cougars equals fewer cougar attacks. Fine presentation of the dilemma cougars (bears and wolves) pose for government agencies and park managers: If you kill a cougar just because it was spotted beside a trail and didn't flee from people, there will be a public outcry claiming it really wasn't necessary to destroy the animal. If you don't kill

the same animal and four days later a cougar—any cougar—in the same
area attacks someone, your agency will get sued. One note of caution
about *Cat Attacks:* It includes a lot of gruesome details about each victim's
injuries.

Montana Department of Fish, Wildlife and Parks. *Living with Montana Mountain
Lions.*

Soussan, Tania. "Woman Encounters Mexican Wolves." *Albuquerque Journal,* May
17, 2000.

CHAPTER 4. COYOTES

California Department of Fish and Game. "Living with California Coyotes."

Washington Department of Fish and Wildlife. "Living with Wildlife in Washington: Coyotes."

CHAPTER 5. GRIZZLY BEARS

Herrero, Stephen. *Bear Attacks: Their Causes and Avoidance.* Revised ed. Guilford,
Conn.: Lyons Press, 2002.

"Staying Safe in Bear Country." Produced by John Hechtel. 50 min. Safety in
Bear Country Society, International Association for Bear Research and
Management, 2001. In this video Alaska Department of Fish and Game
biologist John Hechtel provides the most accurate and up-to-date information available. Great footage of bears interacting with each other and
people. Reviewed by dozens of bear experts.

Smith, Tom S., a biologist with the USGS Alaska Biological Science Center, has
a database on human–bear encounters in Alaska and excellent information on bear safety.

Yellowstone National Park. "Bears and Menstruating Women." Available at
www.nps.gov/yell.

CHAPTER 6. JAVELINAS

Caras, Roger A. *Dangerous to Man: The Definitive Story of Wildlife's Reputed
Dangers.* New York: Henry Holt & Company, 1975.

Heffelfinger, Jim. "Javelina Hunting." Available at *www.javelinahunter.com.*
Heffelfinger is an Arizona Region 5 game specialist.

CHAPTER 7. MOOSE

Alaska Department of Fish and Game, "What to Do About Aggressive Moose."

Washington Department of Fish and Game, "Living With Wildlife in Washington: Moose."

CHAPTER 8. WOLVES

Albuquerque Journal. May 17, 2000, Tania Soussan.

International Wolf Center. "Are Wolves Dangerous to Humans?" Available at *www.wolf.org.* L. David Mech and other wolf biologists are involved with the International Wolf Center. It's one of the few websites about wolves you can trust for accurate information.

McNay, Mark E. "A Case History of Wolf–Human Encounters in Alaska and Canada." Alaska Department of Fish and Game Wildlife Technical Bulletin No. 13, 2002. This carefully worded, objective, unbiased report will give most people new insights about wolves.

Mech, L. David, ed. *The Wolves of Minnesota.* Stillwater, Minn.: Voyageur Press, 2000.

"Wily Wolves Elude Curious Scientists." *Anchorage Alaska Daily News,* September 1, 2002. Discusses Denali National Park's campground wolves.

CHAPTER 9. RABIES

The Centers for Disease Control and Prevention has an excellent website for kids that provides accurate, easy-to-understand information about rabies *(www.cdc.gov).* In addition, some state health departments have solid information on rabies.

THE MOUNTAINEERS, founded in 1906, is a nonprofit outdoor activity and conservation club, whose mission is "to explore, study, preserve, and enjoy the natural beauty of the outdoors. . . . " Based in Seattle, Washington, the club is now the third-largest such organization in the United States, with 15,000 members and five branches throughout Washington State.

The Mountaineers sponsors both classes and year-round outdoor activities in the Pacific Northwest, which include hiking, mountain climbing, ski-touring, snowshoeing, bicycling, camping, kayaking and canoeing, nature study, sailing, and adventure travel. The club's conservation division supports environmental causes through educational activities, sponsoring legislation, and presenting informational programs. All club activities are led by skilled, experienced volunteers, who are dedicated to promoting safe and responsible enjoyment and preservation of the outdoors.

If you would like to participate in these organized outdoor activities or the club's programs, consider a membership in The Mountaineers. For information and an application, write or call The Mountaineers, Club Headquarters, 300 Third Avenue West, Seattle, WA 98119; 206-284-6310.

The Mountaineers Books, an active, nonprofit publishing program of the club, produces guidebooks, instructional texts, historical works, natural history guides, and works on environmental conservation. All books produced by The Mountaineers Books fulfill the club's mission.

Send or call for our catalog of more than 500 outdoor titles:

The Mountaineers Books
1001 SW Klickitat Way, Suite 201
Seattle, WA 98134
800-553-4453
mbooks@mountaineersbooks.org
www.mountaineersbooks.org

The Mountaineers Books is proud to be a corporate sponsor of Leave No Trace, whose mission is to promote and inspire responsible outdoor recreation through education, research, and partnerships. The Leave No Trace program is focused specifically on human-powered (nonmotorized) recreation.

Leave No Trace strives to educate visitors about the nature of their recreational impacts, as well as offer techniques to prevent and minimize such impacts. Leave No Trace is best understood as an educational and ethical program, not as a set of rules and regulations.

For more information, visit *www.LNT.org,* or call 800-332-4100.